HARD
Truths

A One-Month
Devotional

*For those
unwilling to turn away.*

MEEKE ADDISON

Acknowledgments

I deserve death and eternal separation from the God of creation. Because of the sacrifice of Jesus Christ, I have been brought near to God. Thank you Jesus for changing my destiny with one sufficient act of obedience. My first acknowledgment must be of the God who saved me, graced me to know Him, and compels me to make Him known. Without Jesus I am nothing…really…nothing.

Without the encouragement of my husband and best friend, Wil, I might have never ventured to do much of what brings me so much joy. Thank you, Wil, for supporting my call to minister to women. Thank you for suggesting radio. Thank you for not only encouraging my writing but for providing the time and space to do it. You have shown me what godly leadership is. You continue to teach me how to fear God and shun evil. Thank you for not viewing my gifts as threats to your manhood. Thank you for shaping what I'm called to do. I love you more than I could have ever imagined. You're my king.

Moriah, Gabbi, J.D., and Nathaniel oh how I love you! You fill my heart with such joy and hope. I'm thankful for the blessings that you are. You are gracious children and I appreciate your allowing me to write. I'm excited about what God has prepared in advance for you to do as followers of Jesus Christ. Our little arrows.

We're blessed if we have at least one person who knows us and yet loves us anyway. How does one process two? Lane you are so dear to me. You have been my dearest friend for over 15 years and I'm a better friend in general because of you. Without your love and best-friendship I might not have been able to endure several unbearably hard times in my life. I treasure you like a once upon a time experience. Before your friendship, I thought family was defined by blood. I was wrong. You are my sister.

Thank God for my family. All of you. I might fill a separate book to recount all of the blessings and sacrifices that go into working as a unit. Thanks for the last minute trips that make ministry possible. Thanks for your support and encouragement as you've trusted so many times that Wil and I are seeking the Lord and following His lead. Thanks to both of our moms. Mama Sharon, you have been our rock and constant. You listen, encourage, and intercede for our family thank you for always being there is so many ways. We feel your love and send it right back. Mama Dee, thank you for raising me to know the Lord. Thank you for reading the writings of an eight-year-old and treasuring them as instant classics. Mom, you raised five children alone…I didn't know what that meant until now. I love you!

Melonie you're not just my wonderful editor, you're a cherished friend. You get me and I appreciate it. Thanks for making me appear smarter. Thank you Abe for adding your insight and biblical integrity to this book. God has given you an extraordinary mind. Thank you TJ, Randall, and Cortney for asking me incessantly about writing. I see your faces often when at my computer. To my friends who asked me to write a devotional, this is for you. I appreciate you.

Finally, I must acknowledge my AFA family. I can't think of any other place I'd rather labor than alongside men and women who love God, fear Him, and are unapologetic about His standard. Hard truths? It's just what we do.

Foreword

O God, You have cast us off;
You have broken us down;
You have been displeased;
Oh, restore us again!
You have made the earth tremble;
You have broken it;
Heal its breaches, for it is shaking.
You have shown Your people hard things;
You have made us drink the wine of confusion.
— *Psalm 60:1-3 (NKJV)*

"*You* ou have shown Your people hard things." The psalmist's pleas foreshadow the cries of God's covenant people in our troubled times. He continues to show His people hard things – through His eternal, infallible Word; through a world awash in rebellion against His truths; through a self-centered culture immersed in moral anarchy; through a church stumbling and often failing to uphold His truths. Hard things, indeed!

Fortunately, a small army of voices continues to hold up the biblical standard of truths as spelled out in God's Word. Meeke Addison is one of those courageous soldiers in this culture war.

Personally, I'm excited to see this small volume in print. As a coworker of hers at American Family Association, I have sometimes been ungracious as I persistently pushed her to write. But there's a reason I did that – you'll see.

Wherever her voice is heard – on the podium at national conferences, at church events, on the air at Urban Family Talk, on American Family Association's blogsite **The Stand** – Meeke is the epitome of a woman of God. She is committed first to Him, then to her marriage, her four children, her ministry, her church, her friends, our nation.

Hers is an articulate, bold, and unashamed voice upholding God's truths. I commend to you this collection of moving devotions from an avid Christ-follower. Read them start to finish, read them daily, re-read them often. But remember, they are hard truths. Prepare to be challenged and motivated.

Randall Murphree, Editor AFA Journal
American Family Association

Introduction

*T*he feeding of the 5,000 with a couple of small fish and five loaves of bread is an incredible and well-known miracle performed by Jesus Christ. In fact, it's so incredible that it's the only miracle performed by our Lord that is recorded in all four of the gospels. And each account highlights a different aspect of that moment.

Matthew tells us that Jesus had just learned of the beheading of his cousin, John. In that moment of immense grief, Jesus steals away to be alone—possibly to mourn; possibly to pray; most likely to do both, though the Bible doesn't say. The Bible *does* say that Jesus was interrupted by multitudes who followed Him. And rather than turn them away as He grieved, He was moved with compassion for them and healed their sick (Matthew 14:14).

Mark, like Matthew, tells us of the murder of John the Baptist and of the disciples reporting it to Jesus, but he adds that Jesus encouraged the disciples, who had just buried John, to get away to a deserted place that they also might rest for a while. Mark recalls the gathering of the multitude and teaches us that Jesus' compassion not only translated to a desire to heal, but also to a desire to teach. "[Jesus] was moved with compassion for them, because they were like sheep not having a shepherd. So He began to teach them many things" (Mark 6:34).

In addition to the miracle of feeding so many people with so little food, Luke tells us of Jesus' renown, even with Herod the tetrarch. As Jesus continued to perform various miracles, pointing men and women to eternal life, Herod was perplexed. Knowing he had beheaded John the Baptist, he is recorded in Luke 9:9 to have wondered of Jesus, "Who is this of whom I hear such things?" Interestingly, as Luke wanted us to know of even Herod's wondering about Jesus, in all of man's wondering, he can know nothing of Jesus if he doesn't know, as Peter declared, that Jesus is "the Christ of God."

Finally, there is John's account, which neither tells us about the recent beheading of John the Baptist nor of Jesus' retreat for rest or mourning. He also does not tell us about Herod's wondering about the identity of this miracle-working Jesus. What John *does* present to us is one of the saddest exchanges we read about between man and Jesus: The sorrowful condition of man's heart. John's version of Jesus feeding 5,000 people shows the real problem of humanity and our desire for loaves over love. In the Gospel according to John, we learn that the multitude, to whom Jesus has just taught life-giving truths and performed innumerable miracles, including feeding them until full, is still unable to bear the *hard truths* of Christ the Messiah.

Not much has changed since the accounts of Matthew, Mark, Luke, and John. Man still wants what Christ has to offer until He offers line-in-the-sand truth. Our dramatically secular culture promotes popular preachers and soft approaches to moral absolutes. As a result, many professing Christians run dramatically toward the Jesus who fills us with bread in the form of money, cars, or our best life now. But at the very moment Jesus presents *Himself* as the Bread, we turn away, refusing to be satisfied with anything less than what our flesh can feel.

Jesus said then, as He does now, that He is the Bread of Life; all who come to Him and will have eternal life must eat

His flesh and drink His blood (John 6:51, 53). Sadly, many still say, "This is a hard saying; who can understand it?" The message and exclusivity of Christ are a stumbling block to many. Today, possibly more than in any other recent generation, we're witnessing a remarkable turning away. Rare is the Christian who answers as Peter did, despite the cultural pull, "Lord, to whom shall we go? You have the words of eternal life. Also we have come to believe and know that you are the Christ, the Son of the living God."

With Peter's conviction, let us hold the line and double down on the hard truths of God's Word. May we never stumble over the application of Scripture to everyday living, and may we always find ourselves on the Lord's side as we are established in culture.

Day 1

Our foremost community is the Body of Christ.

*R*ecently there has been much talk about communities. We talk about the black community, the white community, or the Latino community. With all the discussion and some of the resulting tension, it would be easy for one to nestle down and filter all information through what is presumed to be one's primary community. However, before we quickly assume our chief identity is anything other than a new creation in Christ, we might need to reevaluate.

What does the Bible teach us about our community? Who does the Bible identify as our family? For the believer, the answer is unequivocally the Body of Christ. Understandably, we may exist in many communities during the course of life. However, in any context, no matter what, our allegiance and solidarity must always be to the Lord and His people—those who profess Christ. And no matter what, our operation within any context may never extend beyond the limitations of the Word of God.

I'm a wife, a mother, and a black American, but none of that extends with any prominence into eternity. Our greatest identification is follower of Christ, and as such, our highest allegiance is to Him and the community He carves out.

Matthew 12:46-50, Romans 8:15, 29; 2 Corinthians 5:17

For whom He foreknew, He also predestined to be con-formed to the image of His Son, that He might be the first-born among many brethren. –Romans 8:29

_____

_____

_____

_____

_____

_____

_____

_____

_____

_____

_____

_____

_____

_____

_____

_____

_____

_____

_____

_____

_____

_____

_____

_____

_____

_____

_____

Day 2

We are *not* all God's children.

*W*e are all made in the image of God, and our value derives from that. However, somewhere along the way, someone thought it was a good idea to ascribe to all of creation son-ship with God as our Father. The fact that we are made in the image of God is a characteristic that would be true whether we accept Christ or not, but the identity of son-ship is one reserved only for those who have accepted the sacrifice of Jesus Christ.

There is a huge difference between being made in the image of God and being a child of God. The children of God have the Holy Spirit indwelling them. He is the seal of God which guarantees our inheritance. He marks us. To be a child of God means you are a part of the family of God; you have inherited eternal life. If you are not purchased by Jesus, then you are not a child of God. In fact, the Bible makes it quite clear that those who are not the Lord's have a different father.

Romans 8:12-17; John 8:37-47; Galatians 3:26

For you are all sons of God through faith in Christ Jesus.
–Galatians 3:26 (NKJV)

_____

_____

_____

_____

_____

_____

_____

_____

_____

_____

_____

_____

_____

_____

_____

_____

_____

_____

_____

_____

_____

_____

_____

_____

_____

_____

_____

Day 3

A genuine conversion will result in a necessarily different life.

*S*o many people say they are saved. They are absolutely convinced they have a place in Heaven, but their reasons are hard-pressed to find in the Bible. Let's face it: One has to be a special kind of person to *want* to go to hell. Contrary to popular belief and exhibition, those who have been converted will demonstrate a newness of life. No squinting should be required to recognize true believers; neither should Christians falsely believe that all "good" and moral people are saved.

Interestingly, while all "good" or moral people aren't saved, all saved people should be.

For the Christian, our behavior reflects the work of Jesus Christ in our lives. If you are comfortable in sin, if your life looks exactly as it did prior to your accepting Christ, then it's possible that your experience was an emotional one void of the redemptive work of the Holy Spirit. Unfortunately, this may be a scarier position than outright rejection of Christ.

Romans 8:5-11; Colossians 3:1-11; 1 John 2:3-6

Now by this we know that we know Him, if we keep His commandments. He who says, "I know Him," and does not keep His commandments, is a liar, and the truth is not in him. But whoever keeps His word, truly the love of God is perfected in him. By this we know that we are in Him. He who says he abides in Him ought himself also to walk just as He walked. –1 John 2:3-6

_____

_____

_____

_____

_____

_____

_____

_____

_____

_____

_____

_____

_____

_____

_____

_____

_____

_____

_____

_____

_____

_____

_____

_____

Day 4

The call to follow Christ is still the call to die.

*U*nfortunately, we in America have enjoyed a soft, inclusive Christianity. We can simply add Jesus to our lives as a form of "insurance." If nothing else works, at least I have my "Jesus policy." As a result of our soft approach to Christ, many of us are unable to share in the sufferings of our brothers and sisters throughout the world who are literally losing their lives for the Gospel. We actually can't fathom it as reality.

While a great many of us will never have to choose between our head or our Christ, we are daily faced with either keeping our status, our acceptance, and our employment, or keeping our Christ. The cross we carry on our backs as we follow Jesus Christ must be planted, and we must nail ourselves to it daily. Every time we side with Christ, our flesh dies. When we reject the need to be liked, our flesh dies. When we do what we should instead of what we want, our flesh dies.

The cross to which we nail ourselves is totally different from the ones we wear around our necks. It's not pretty or petite. It's not lightweight. May we never carry our cross for looks. May we ever use it as the gruesome, public method of death for which it was intended.

Matthew 16:24-27; 1 Corinthians 15:31; Philippians 3:8; Galatians 2:20

I affirm, by the boasting in you
which I have in Christ Jesus our Lord, I die daily.
−1 Corinthians 15:31

_____

_____

_____

_____

_____

_____

_____

_____

_____

_____

_____

_____

_____

_____

_____

_____

_____

_____

_____

_____

_____

_____

_____

_____

_____

_____

_____

_____

_____

_____

Day 5

The Church is *not* a social club for good people or those seeking a place to belong.

*N*ot too long ago, someone thought it was a good idea to turn the gathering of the Saints into a party or meeting that the unsaved would like to attend. The hope was that we, the "called out of Christ," would look so cool that those who didn't love God would just want to hang out. Then hopefully, they would eventually hear a type of gospel, and if the lighting was just right, they would give their hearts to Christ.

The privilege of the Christian community is for the Christian. We are talking about the Bride of Christ, the Body of Christ, the Church—*not* a pass-time meeting attended by fine Americans. The Church is for the saved of Christ. To engineer a meeting void of His presence and lite on His Truth is to effectively create a group of good people. There's nothing wrong with a club made up of good people; we just should not call it the Church.

This is a hard truth because we have generations of people that have only known the Church as *the* vehicle of evangelism. *We* the followers of Christ are the evangelists. We are the soul-winners. Certainly we learn, are equipped and empowered within the context of the Church with the purpose of going out to win the lost. The Church and its integrity should never be sacrificed for numbers. Telling people that the Church should "tone it down" is like telling a bride that she should not wear her best on her wedding day so that attendees won't feel badly about themselves or how they're dressed.

Acts 2:40-47; Ephesians 4:11-16

*And He Himself gave some to be apostles, some prophets,
some evangelists, and some pastors and teachers, ^{12} for the
equipping of the saints for the work of ministry, for the edi-
fying of the body of Christ, ^{13} till we all come to the unity of
the faith and of the knowledge of the Son of God, to a perfect
man, to the measure of the stature of the fullness of Christ;
that we should no longer be children, tossed to and fro and
carried about with every wind of doctrine, by the trickery of
men, in the cunning craftiness of deceitful plotting,*
–Ephesians 4:11-14

Day 6

Jesus didn't die to make me a successful person, give me a better home, car, or job.

*M*y happiness isn't guaranteed in the Gospel, neither does it promise that I'll be spared sorrow or loss. The guarantee of the Gospel is that the sacrifice of Jesus Christ is sufficient.

Jesus' work on the cross justified all who would put their hope in Him. His blood covers my past, present, and future sins. The Gospel doesn't promise me a new car, the Gospel doesn't promise me an enviable home, and the Gospel certainly doesn't promise me American success. Admittedly there are perks to being in the family of God. I've avoided certain woes simply because I have submitted fully (though not perfectly) to new life in Christ and His call to holiness. The Gospel is not now, nor has it ever been about living your best life now. The Gospel is about living life eternally with the God who made you.

The good news is Jesus saves. When we reduce the message of the cross to stuff and things, pep talks and self-help, we disrespect the work of God through Jesus Christ. I may live a better life than the enemies of God, but that's a plus—not the promise.

Ephesians 1:13 & 14; Romans 5:1-5; Luke 12:13-21; John 16:33

These things I have spoken to you, that in Me you may have peace. In the world you will have tribulation; but be of good cheer, I have overcome the world. –John 16:33

_____
_____
_____
_____
_____
_____
_____
_____
_____
_____
_____
_____
_____
_____
_____
_____
_____
_____
_____
_____
_____
_____
_____
_____
_____
_____
_____
_____
_____
_____

Day 7

God is not good because I think so. None of my life experiences define His goodness.

*W*henever I hear people say, "God is good because..." and then list all the stuff that worked out in their favor, or when they talk about God giving them the stuff they wanted, I wonder if they would still say God is good if none of that happened or came to them.

It's dangerous for us to classify God as good independent of the fact that He *is* goodness. Without respect to anything He *has* done or *will* do in creation, God *is* good. And what's more, He's better than my best definition of good.

So on a scale of 1-10, 10 being the best measure of God's goodness, He's a pomegranate. Ridiculous, right? As are our attempts to define His goodness.

Measuring God's goodness on a scale created by those whom He has created is futile. To be good by our definition, He could not have suffered His only begotten Son to die for thugs, sinners, and the ungrateful. To be good by our definition, He could never allow our refinement, perfection, or sanctification to come by way of things that cause us great heartache, pain, and grief. To be good by our definition, *no one* would be destroyed, and Heaven would be all-access.

So the next time someone asks, "If God is so good, why does He..." stop them short and teach them that God's goodness is not defined by us. Unlike humans, God doesn't "act good" or do good things. No—God *is* good. To be sure, it's a good we'll only understand fully in eternity.

Isaiah 53:10 & 11; 2 Corinthians 5:21; Psalm 100:4 & 5

For the Lord is good;
His mercy is everlasting,
And His truth endures to all generations. –Psalm 100:5

_____

_____

_____

_____

_____

_____

_____

_____

_____

_____

_____

_____

_____

_____

_____

_____

_____

_____

_____

_____

_____

_____

_____

_____

_____

_____

_____

_____

Day 8

Not a small number of people I care for dearly and love deeply will go to hell.

*W*hen I think about this fact, my eyes burn with tears. I have family and friends who reject Jesus and His available forgiveness. I have family and friends who play an excellent role of "believer," but they are far from God.

Many people live as if hell is some sort of fairy tale invented by parents to keep their kids in line. Others act as if they are too charming or spiritual for God to send them to hell. And still, others believe hell is not an actual place, but a state of being—something a good therapist could fix.

Hell *is* a real place. Yes—an actual, physical place that has enlarged itself in preparation for some of my friends and family. My heart is heavy at the typing of this truth. The call now is for men and women everywhere to confess their sins, repent, and receive the justification that comes only from the work of our Savior, Jesus on the cross. I want people everywhere to be spared destruction.

Full disclosure: I experience a special grief when I think about people I know personally and love deeply rejecting the Lord. Yet even in this, God *is* good.

Matthew 7: 13 & 14; Matthew 25:31-46; Matthew 13:47-51; Isaiah 5:12-16; Revelation 21:8

Therefore Sheol has enlarged itself
And opened its mouth beyond measure;
Their glory and their multitude and their pomp,
And he who is jubilant, shall descend into it.
People shall be brought down,
Each man shall be humbled,
And the eyes of the lofty shall be humbled.
But the Lord of hosts shall be exalted in judgment,
And God who is holy shall be hallowed in righteousness.
–Isaiah 5:14-16

Day 9

There are wolves among us.

*T*he wolves in the Christian community are ravenous. The wolves are in positions of influence and leadership. They look like excellent Christian leaders. They are well spoken and emotional. They write well and motivate people to move mountains. But at their core, they are agents of the devil.

Wolves teach, by various methods, destructive doctrines, principles, or tenets. Wolves would be easier to spot if they were all of the David Koresh or Jim Jones persuasion, but as it is, they are more Little Bo Peep or Winnie the Pooh. You trust them, you read their stuff, and you adopt most of it. But in the end, they have propagated destruction. These people are attractive and popular, and they spew convincing words. You're drawn to them because what they say "makes sense."

When wolves speak or write, many mistake for Holy Spirit confirmation what is quite simply a flesh massage. There is no defense against the destruction of persuasive wolves except *the holy Word of God*. Wolves are afraid of the Bible, and of the people who read it for that matter. Wolves don't ever want you to check their facts or read above or below the Scripture verses they loosely use. They are masters of object lessons, topical sermons, and soft understandings of hard truths. You may be in the presence of a wolf if he bristles when you seek clarity on a point he makes or a position he holds.

The Saints of God must know the Word. Read it daily. Read it contextually. Read it to be searched and changed.

2 Peter 2:1-3 & 18-22; Romans 16:17-20; Matthew 7:15- 23

But there were also false prophets among the people, even as there will be false teachers among you, who will secretly bring in destructive heresies, even denying the Lord who bought them, and bring on themselves swift destruction. And many will follow their destructive ways, because of whom the way of truth will be blasphemed. By covetousness they will exploit you with deceptive words; for a long time their judgment has not been idle, and their destruction does not slumber.
–2 Peter 2:1-3

Day 10

We're supposed to judge those who claim Christ.

*W*hen a brother or sister in Christ sins and is unrepentant, it actually *is* our business. It would be so much easier for us to put our heads down and blissfully wait for His return when we come to Christ, but as it is, we Christians are called to engage the Body. Like it or not (and most don't), we are accountable to one another. It's just true. God uses us in each other's lives to aid in the sanctification process. It's in community that we grow and conform to Christ. It's supposed to be in community that we are called to repentance when we sin and restored when we repent.

Sadly, the Church listens to the world, which says, "You can't judge." Christian, that is and isn't what the Bible teaches believers. If a brother or sister in Christ is immoral and loving it, we are not only charged to judge the matter, we are also admonished to not even keep company with that person. What?! The problem is, as the president of my organization puts it, "We want to be better than Jesus." So we ignore Scripture in hopes of being well-liked.

We have an epidemic of Christians behaving badly, but worse than that, we have a growing number of Christians who choose to look in the other direction. Both are missing the mark. Left unchecked, sin spreads like wildfire or leaven. Is someone in unrepentant sin around you? Judge it. Say what the Lord says about sin. Meet with that person. Call him or her to repentance. When they repent walk with them and restore them. However if they refuse to repent, "put away from yourselves the evil person."

Psalm 1; 1 Corinthians 5:9-13; Galatians 6:1-5; Matthew 7:1-5

But now I have written to you not to keep company with anyone named a brother, who is sexually immoral, or covetous, or an idolater, or a reviler, or a drunkard, or an extortioner—not even to eat with such a person.
−1 Corinthians 5:11

_____
_____
_____
_____
_____
_____
_____
_____
_____
_____
_____
_____
_____
_____
_____
_____
_____
_____
_____
_____
_____
_____
_____
_____
_____

Day 11

Amassing many possessions or enjoying a popular or successful life doesn't always mean you have the Lord's seal of approval.

Sometimes I get in trouble introspectively when I try to consider why the Lord allows the wicked to flourish in wickedness. I mean, I'm downright upset when I see the wicked flaunting their sin. With the same mouth they use to curse God, they say He has blessed them. I often think, *Lord take it away and humble them. They blaspheme you and then say you're blessing them.* I get angry (sorry to admit that). I think, *Lord, but you can show them you're in control.*

And then I'm reminded by the Holy Spirit and the Word that He *is* in control. And to be rich or successful in this life is not a safe way to determine that the Lord approves of you.

We in the Body of Christ who have believed the lie that our status in this life is directly connected to our standing with God, must reject that and return to a complete knowledge of the Word. Those of us who love God and are ransomed by Jesus experience loss, need, and yes—physical poverty. Meanwhile, those who make sport of sin seem to experience no lack.

Does God sometimes use physical or financial loss to grab the attention of His people? Absolutely! In like manner, He can also reward the choices we make to honor Him with success and various degrees of comfort.

The caution here is important: If our sole way of measuring our justification is by what we have, do, or achieve, then there will be many surprised people at the end of this age.

Luke 12:15-21; Ecclesiastes 7:13-15; James 2:5

Listen, my beloved brethren: Has God not chosen the poor of this world to be rich in faith and heirs of the kingdom which He promised to those who love Him? –James 2:5

_____

_____

_____

_____

_____

_____

_____

_____

_____

_____

_____

_____

_____

_____

_____

_____

_____

_____

_____

_____

_____

_____

_____

_____

_____

_____

_____

_____

_____

_____

Day 12

If the world loves you, then there is probably enmity between you and God.

*E*nmity: The state or feeling of being actively opposed or hostile to someone or something.

When we recall Jesus' warnings about our acceptance by the world, the phrase "popular pastor" seems to almost be a contradiction of terms. I don't enjoy being hated; I don't know very many people who do. But Jesus told us that we (Christians) would be. So how is it possible that there are so many world-loved believers? I'm convinced it's because there's so much compromise.

Think about the reasons the world hated Jesus. These are supposed to be all the same reasons it hates us. Jesus was not of this world, and neither should we be. The world didn't know the One by whom Jesus was sent, and neither do they know the One to whom we submit. Jesus reminded the world of their sin (still does). Likewise, our righteous living and pressing for holiness convict the world that there is no excuse for sin.

In order for the world to love us, we'd have to undertake some intentional practices. For one thing, we'd have to look less like Christ. We'd have to lower the standards of holiness. We'd have to deny there are any requirements of righteousness from God. But if even one of these factors is present, there is certainly enmity, strife between you and God. We're not above Jesus, so we can't be loved by the world more than Jesus was or is.

The disciples rejoiced that they were counted worthy to suffer shame for the name of Jesus. You never see even one rejoice for being able to fly under the radar and barely even be identified as a follower of the Way. If being loved and celebrated by the world is your aim, then loving and celebrating Jesus isn't. They are mutually exclusive.

John 15:18-25; Matthew 10:22; Acts 5:41; 1 John 2:15 James 4:4

Adulterers and adulteresses! Do you not know that friendship with the world is enmity with God? Whoever therefore wants to be a friend of the world makes himself an enemy of God.
–James 4:4

Day 13

Cowards are never celebrated in Scripture.

*M*aybe someone started a rumor that Christians should be non-confrontational. Or maybe someone wrote a book about us staying inside the four walls of our churches and hunkering down until Jesus cracks the skies. However it happened, we now have at least two generations (maybe more) of comfortable cowards—that with absolutely no biblical support.

It doesn't matter how many trendy synonyms we find to refresh the word "coward," the actions are all the same. So whether you call it "relevant," "seeker-sensitive," "tolerant," "inclusive," "progressive," or "post-modern," if it serves as a means by which to avoid addressing sin, unrighteousness, or wickedness—especially for fear of being rejected—then it's just plain, old cowardice.

The Bible lists the cowardly among the unbelieving, abominable, murderers, sexually immoral, sorcerers, idolaters, and liars—for all of whom the final destination is hell. Paul lamented being abandoned by cowards; "No one stood with me," he said. But knowing the fate of cowards, even Paul asked that "it not be charged against them."

Boldness is an evidence of the Holy Spirit who seals us. One could easily make the connection between the cowardly—those destined for hell—and a lack of the presence of the Holy Spirit—the guarantee that we are the Lord's.

2 Timothy 4:16 & 17; Revelation 21:8; Acts 1:8, 4:31; 2 Timothy 1:7 & 8

But the Lord stood with me and strengthened me, so that the message might be preached fully through me, and that all the Gentiles might hear. Also I was delivered out of the mouth of the lion. −2 Timothy 4:17

Day 14

Our failure to uphold the Lord's standards of holiness and righteousness *do not* nullify them.

*I*f we say we have no sin, then we deceive ourselves. And yet the charge for believers everywhere is absolutely to lay aside every weight and the sin which so easily ensnares us. How can both of those be true?

One speaks of the indisputable fact that we are prone to sin; we have a nature of sin. The other speaks of the sanctification process whereby we are transformed by renewed minds and conformed to the image of Christ. So while we know we are not sinless (a distinction only Jesus holds), we also know that by the power of the Holy Spirit we can and should sin less. The trouble arises when we coddle the sin we favor and deceive ourselves into thinking God no longer sees it as such.

So just so we're clear: Fornication is still sin—even if you love him or her. Lying is still sin—even if it makes someone else feel better. Adultery is still sin—even if you're both miserable anyway. Homosexuality is still sin—even if a nation recognizes it as "marriage." Murder is still sin—even if you call it reproductive rights. Gossip is still sin—even if you call it a prayer request. Pride is still sin—even if you call it confidence.

I'm sure others and their soft-titled justifications can be added to this list. The point is we're not powerful or smooth enough to change God's mind regarding His standards. His standard is *the* standard. In fact, our failure to meet the standard reaffirms the holiness of God. It also confirms the fact that we deserve hell. Thank God for Jesus!

Hebrews 12:1; James 1:21-25; Romans 7; 1 Peter 1:16

Therefore lay aside all filthiness and overflow of wicked-
ness, and receive with meekness the implanted word,
which is able to save your souls. –James 1:21

_____
_____
_____
_____
_____
_____
_____
_____
_____
_____
_____
_____
_____
_____
_____
_____
_____
_____
_____
_____
_____
_____
_____
_____
_____
_____
_____
_____
_____
_____

Day 15

We have freedom in Christ.

*T*his could appear to be an easy truth. It's not. Freedom reveals the heart in a way that keeping rules can't. I'm moved by my children when I see their obedience in submission to my rules. However, I learn more about the condition of their little hearts when they are given a choice and choose to act in a way that is consistent with their profession of faith. I watch for it.

The freedom we have in Christ is for freedom, but it must not be used as a cover-up for sin. Quite often we prefer rules because our hearts are not knit to God. We find ourselves squinting at, even perplexed by, those "disputable matters" of which the Apostle Paul wrote. Sometimes we want the rules. We feel safe inside the lines. When I consider that my unapologetic love for my husband makes rules virtually unnecessary, how much more should my incomparable love for God drive me toward Him and away from sin and indulgence?

Don't taste, don't touch, don't look, and other such rules may help us *look* Christian, but God's Holy Spirit actually helps us behave Christian—from the inside out. Without the Holy Spirit, freedom is a stumbling block. However, with Him, freedom is a building block serving to mature us. Maybe it's by design, but it's quite possible that freedom is one of the greatest disclosures of the condition of a man's heart.

Colossians 2:20-23; Romans 14:1-13; 1 Peter 2:15 & 16; Galatians 5:13

For you, brethren, have been called to liberty; only do not use liberty as an opportunity for the flesh, but through love serve one another. –Galatians 5:13

Day 16

Our interpersonal relationships matter to God.

*S*ometimes we're just one disagreement away from putting people in the "done with you" category. But unless there is clear, unrepentant sin, we will not find any Scripture to support our desertion of our brothers and sisters in Christ.

I've had strong disagreements with siblings in the Lord, and I have even put them away mentally and emotionally. And yet at the very moment I feel relieved to not have to deal with them anymore, I feel the strong conviction of the Holy Spirit imploring me to be reconciled.

Real talk: I've tried to imagine what it would be like to be in Heaven with people I just don't like. How ridiculous! As believers, we have a different element to our relationships. We're not just friends; we're family. And as such we have that "can't get away from them" connection.

Our relationships within the Body matter so much that they affect our relationship with the Lord. I've read it, but worse, still I've felt it. I know what it feels like to have interrupted fellowship with the Lord because of a break in fellowship with another believer. Division within the Body is a device of the evil one. Division spreads like the flu, and ultimately, the world mocks our faith when they see their dysfunction among those who claim Christ.

For the sake of other believers, our communion with God, and the integrity of the faith, we must ensure that regular and genuine reconciliation takes place in our circles.

What strained relationship needs your attention?

Matthew 5:23 & 24; 1 John 4:20 &21; Ephesians 4:32; 1 Corinthians 1:10 & 11

And be kind to one another, tenderhearted, forgiving one another, even as God in Christ forgave you.
–Ephesians 4:32

_____

_____

_____

_____

_____

_____

_____

_____

_____

_____

_____

_____

_____

_____

_____

_____

_____

_____

_____

_____

_____

_____

_____

_____

_____

_____

_____

_____

_____

Day 17

The enemies of God are my enemies.

*W*hen I was in elementary school and my classmates got into arguments on the playground, all the kids were left to figure out where they stood as a result of the spat. If two friends "fell out," we were always left to decide whose side we were on. Oh, those childhood woes. I'm so glad life in Christ is much easier.

Without apology, the enemies of God—those who vehemently oppose Him and those who mock His people because of our faith—are absolutely, 100 percent my enemies! I'm always on the Lord's side. My opposition to those who oppose God does not allow for a lot of niceties. It's not funny to me when the world mocks the Lord. It's not funny to me when Christians "see where 'they' are coming from."

Who laughs while someone verbally abuses their children? What husband do you know who would look away as his wife is spat upon when it was within his power to act? I personally don't know many. Likewise, I find it weak and inexcusable for Christians to always understand the world's woes versus communicating the truth of God's Word. I'm confused by professing Christians who always seek the world's acceptance and approval while the Saints endure increasing oppression and mockery.

Incidentally, loving my enemies while still considering them my enemy creates no contradiction for me. We must read contextually. When we do, we'll discover that we too were the enemies of God and yet graciously loved by Him.

Psalm 139:20-22; Mark 13:13; Matthew 10:34-36; 1 Kings 18:21; Romans 5:10

Do not think that I came to bring peace on earth. I did not come to bring peace but a sword. For I have come to 'set a man against his father, a daughter against her mother, and a daughter-in-law against her mother-in-law'; and 'a man's enemies will be those of his own household.
–Matthew 10:34-36

_____

_____

_____

_____

_____

_____

_____

_____

_____

_____

_____

_____

_____

_____

_____

_____

_____

_____

_____

_____

_____

_____

_____

_____

_____

_____

_____

Day 18

What we believe is illogical.

*L*et's face it—when we try to tell people what we believe, we communicate it 100 percent by faith. If you've ever shared your faith with an un-churched person, you're familiar with the look on that person's face. It reminds you that what you believe is spiritually revealed.

Recap: God, whom we can't see, exists eternally (no end/ no beginning). He made everything we see. He created two people, and all of humanity comes from them. They sinned and passed sin on to all of us. Sin makes us an enemy of the God we can't see, but God was merciful and chose to forgive our sin. So, a young, virgin girl conceived a son whose Father is the eternally existent God who made her. He was sinless because He was not born of the flesh yet grew in a womb. He died as a sacrifice for us and was raised again after three days. His blood saves us from a literal hell. He is alive in Heaven (an actual place), seated at the right hand of the God who required His sacrifice for our sake. He will come back and take all of us who simply believe in His name to be with Him forever.

WHAT? Yes! There's more, but you usually don't get to all of it.

So how do we who believe this arrive at this belief? The Holy Spirit. The Holy Spirit convicts us of sin. The Holy Spirit confirms what we hear. He is the One who says to you, "This is true." He says, "Repent." He says, "Draw near to God."

Understanding this hard truth creates an incredible amount of humility, because we realize that we are not saved because we were smart enough to get it. We realize that we are not saved because we have a wonderfully wild imagination. No—we realize that we are saved because the Holy Spirit drew us, and the day we heard His voice, we didn't harden our hearts. As we share the gospel, and as we watch the world increasingly mock what we believe, we should be humbled, as it becomes undeniably clear that God's love and mercy have drawn us to the saving knowledge of Jesus Christ.

If the faith makes sense to you, then you can rest assured that it has been revealed to you by the Holy Spirit. It's not because you're smart enough or good enough to get it.

John 6:45, 15:26, 16:5-15; 1 Corinthians 1:18-21

It is written in the prophets, 'And they shall all be taught by God.' Therefore everyone who has heard and learned from the Father comes to Me. –John 6:45

_____

_____

_____

_____

_____

_____

_____

_____

_____

_____

_____

_____

_____

_____

_____

_____

_____

_____

_____

_____

_____

_____

_____

_____

_____

_____

_____

_____

_____

Day 19

Before the throne of Christ's judgment, everyone will receive exactly what he or she deserves.

About three years ago, a Christian friend of mine told me that even if he were to be sent eternally to hell at the end of his life, he would know that he had received exactly what he deserved. God is just.

I have never forgotten that conversation, it forced me to search myself for that same conviction. We deal with humans – that's a given. We're used to human error or mistakes. Unfortunately, as a result of that fact, we may be tempted to think that God could or would make a mistake... especially in dealing with us.

The bottom line is this: God is just. He is always right. He never makes mistakes. Whatever He determines to do is consistent with His nature and the fact that He is just. So with regard to our loved ones, and even with regard to ourselves, God deals justly. There is no perspective that matters apart from what God determines. We have no right to approach Him and demand fairness. The notion of fairness is subjective and requires comparison. God is not fair; He is just. He is the ultimate straightedge.

If, after all I've done seemingly for God, I were to be eternally damned, I have learned enough to both mourn the loss of eternal fellowship with the God who made me and to accept what I received as God's perfect justice.

It's difficult for me to use that example. Oh, merciful God, thank you for Jesus!

Genesis 18:25; 2 Corinthians 5:9-11; Galatians 6:7 & 8; Matthew 7:21-23

For we must all appear before the judgment seat of Christ,
that each one may receive the things done in the body,
according to what he has done, whether good or bad.
–2 Corinthians 5:10

_____

_____

_____

_____

_____

_____

_____

_____

_____

_____

_____

_____

_____

_____

_____

_____

_____

_____

_____

_____

_____

_____

_____

_____

_____

_____

_____

Day 20

The Holy Spirit does NOT lead people into sin.

"God told me" is one of the most flippant and abused assertions Christians make. We credit God with any and everything.

"God told me to leave my husband for a man who 'completes' me." Or "God told me to remove teaching about sin from my sermons." Or, one of my personal favorites, "God told me you're my wife." (Bless my sweet friend who recently told me about a gentleman who tells her this regularly.)

I'm sure you've heard many others.

If the Lord leads you to do something, then it should fit within the parameters of His holy Word, and there should be other mature believers to confirm what you're sensing. If those conditions are not met, then don't credit God with it. Just say you *feel* or you *desire*. It's dangerous to say God told you to do something that isn't supported biblically. The Word of God is the litmus test for what we hear in our hearts.

If we are free to say, "God told me," and expect it to have the same weight as Scripture, then there is nothing to stop us from forming cults. There is no barricade between doctrine and "new revelation." We must test all things. We do that with the straight-edge of the holy Word of God. Of course there are daily events in life where the Lord leads us, and we make decisions that glorify Him as a result. We call that walking in the Spirit. But we must take special care to ensure that we don't abuse the leading of the Spirit by claiming He has led us to do self-serving, questionable, or even sinful things. With such behavior, God is not pleased.

We must revere God and take great care with the use of His name. He is holy, and who is bold enough to misrepresent the eternal, self-existent One?

1 Thessalonians 5:16-22; James 1:13-18; 2 Timothy 3:16 & 17; 2 Peter 1:20 &21; Proverbs 30:5 & 6

Test all things; hold fast what is good.
Abstain from every form of evil. –1 Thessalonians 5:21

Day 21

Actually, *God* sees color.

*I*f a person says, "I don't see color," I understand immediately what he means. Translation: I'm not making
any judgments about your character based solely on the color
of your skin. And that's a good thing.

A bad thing is pretending or hoping we could all just get
over the color of people's skin. To try to avoid our uniqueness
and the beauty of it is to miss completely an aspect of God's
creativity in creation. Avoiding color is a lofty goal, but it is
not a biblical one. A better goal is to *see* color and worship
our Creator for the wonderful works His hand has made.

Sin has distorted our view of humanity, and all of creation
for that matter. Sin causes hatred of another person based
solely on skin color, ethnicity, or nationality. The Body of
Christ should be the greatest example of what Heaven will
look like because we have come to understand how dividing
walls have been abolished at conversion. If the recognition
of skin color or ethnicity were sinful, then we should expect
it to be eradicated in Heaven. But to the contrary, according
to John and what he saw, it's all over Heaven.

When I see your color, I'm reminded of just how awe-
some God is. "Set apart" means being distinct in all aspects
of Christian living, including the navigation of relationships
across cultural lines.

Galatians 3:27 & 28; Revelation 5:8-10, 7:9, Acts 17:26 & 27

And they sang a new song, saying:
"You are worthy to take the scroll,
And to open its seals;
For You were slain,
And have redeemed us to God by Your blood
Out of every tribe and tongue and people and nation,
[10] And have made us kings and priests to our God;
And we shall reign on the earth." –Revelation 5: 9 &10

_____

_____

_____

_____

_____

_____

_____

_____

_____

_____

_____

_____

_____

_____

_____

_____

_____

_____

_____

_____

_____

_____

_____

_____

Day 22

God does not *need* me.

*B*ecause we've resorted to gimmicks to boost conversion numbers, we've crafted a Savior that would be unrecognizable to the first century Church. Today's Jesus is either desperate for people to believe in Him or incomplete without us coming to faith in him. This is man's design, and it is utterly false, yet we rarely question it because it positions us at the center of the universe.

With the utmost respect to who we are in creation—the distinction between us and animals, our new identity in Christ, our ability to have fellowship with God, etc.—God does not need us. He is not hopeless without us. He wasn't lonely before He created us. There is no void in God that we fill. God is not powerless if *we* don't act. God doesn't need our permission to do *anything* in the Earth.

God is omnipotent. He *is* all powerful. He chose to create us because it pleased Him to do so. He chose to reveal who He is to us through the creation account, through the chronicling of man's history, and through allowing us to recognize our need for redemption. None of what we have been allowed to learn about our history supports the belief that we complete God. The eternally existent Godhead is complete; in Him there is no lack. So on the contrary *we* are complete in Him.

Yes—God loves us with an everlasting love! This is demonstrated in His providing a way for us to be reconciled to Himself though Jesus. But He didn't do that because He was empty without us. The pleasure, the privilege, and the benefits of coming to God are all ours. You're pretty special. I'm kinda special too. But none of us is special enough that we "fixed" God because we accepted Christ. What a mighty God we serve! He loves us with an incomprehensible love, and yet He doesn't need us. Nope—not one bit.

Colossians 2:8-10; Psalm 50:8-15; Isaiah 43:13; Luke 19:37-40

Beware lest anyone cheat you through philosophy and empty deceit, according to the tradition of men, according to the basic principles of the world, and not according to Christ. For in Him dwells all the fullness of the Godhead bodily; and you are complete in Him, who is the head of all principality and power. –Colossians 2:8-10

Day 23

We are *not* basically good.

"*I*'m a good person" is one of the first reasons you will hear unsaved people give for why they should avoid hell. There's been a big push to confirm in nature the "people are basically good" teaching, so we're desperate for viral videos and news stories that point to the "good at our core" conviction.

Again, this teaching is not supported in Scripture. The adoption of this notion by the Church and the Body of Christ is a result of the world influencing the Church versus the Church influencing the world.

We will absolutely come across nice people and people who do good things, but to use that as a support for the secular notion that people are kind of good on their own is eternally destructive. A firm understanding of how sinful and wicked we are is needed if we are to even come to Christ. When I come face-to-face with who I really am, I'm disgusted and run toward the mercy of God. I plead with God because of Christ to save me, forgive me, and cleanse me of sin and the nothing good that dwells in my flesh.

We do people a disservice when we perpetuate the myth that they are good and that Jesus just polishes them up a little. There is no goodness outside the work the Holy Spirit does in our lives. Apart from Christ, our nature is sinful. This is in part the reason why we need to be born again and to put on our new nature, which is Jesus Christ. Nice people don't go to Heaven, and neither do good ones—only those who are perfect. This perfection is only attained in Christ, the propitiation for our sin. Thank God for Jesus!

Romans 7; Genesis 6:5; Galatians 5:17; Ephesians 2:3; Isaiah 6:5; Jeremiah 17:9

And you He made alive, who were dead in trespasses and sins, in which you once walked according to the course of this world, according to the prince of the power of the air, the spirit who now works in the sons of disobedience, among whom also we all once conducted ourselves in the lusts of our flesh, fulfilling the desires of the flesh and of the mind, and were by nature children of wrath, just as the others.
–Ephesians 2:1-3

Day 24

True friends tell you hard truths.

A person who is unwilling to tell you anything other than what you delight to hear doesn't actually love you. The Bible has much to say in support of this.

We have been programmed by the flesh to only want what we want, and as a result, we don't have much room in our lives for discipleship, correction, or loving rebuke. We tend to automatically think that a person who challenges us doesn't love us. But if we filter this belief through Scripture, we'll find the opposite to be true.

How about this: A person who doesn't tell you hard truths loves him or herself.

We often spare people hard truths because we don't want them to be upset with us, we don't want to lose their friendship, or we just can't stand the tension. But a person who loves you deeply will risk or endure all three. It's the ultimate display of selflessness.

I'm willing to be hurt (even by you) if it means your well-being. We must beware people who flatter us with swelling words. And for those who agree with us all the time, we must wonder if those people are truly genuine. I would say if you don't have someone in your life who can speak directly to areas of sin or shortcoming, then you are most likely missing out on growing in critical areas of your walk with the Lord.

The charge is two-fold: We must desire to *speak* the truth, even when it's most difficult, and we must desire to *hear* the truth, even when it's most difficult.

Proverbs 26:24-28, 27:5 & 6, 27:17; Psalm 12:1-3; Colossians 3:9 & 10

A lying tongue hates those who are crushed by it,
And a flattering mouth works ruin. –Proverbs 26:28

Day 25

Purity still matters to God.

*E*ven the word "purity" sounds dated. Many in the Christian community have abandoned teaching and caring about purity in exchange for "how to have a hotter body" or "six absolute ways to turn heads." We've lost our conviction about what it means to live a life of purity before God and our brothers and sisters. We may still teach it to our youth, but as adults, we find it adolescent.

Meanwhile, some of the biggest strongholds in the life of the believer are those that are easily hidden.

Lust is not always immediately obvious, but it has huge spiritual implications for Christians. And while no one is advocating for burlap bags as Christian fashion, we must return to avoiding even the appearance of impropriety.

Contrary to what our culture teaches men and women, we in the Body of Christ have a much higher standard. It's not "okay to look." God still considers that sin. It's not okay to dress in such a way that would cause your brother to sin when he sees you. We have liberty in Christ—yes. But to use liberty as a justification for sensuality is sinful.

Godly women take no joy in causing another woman's husband to sin by desiring her. And Godly men are disgusted by the enemy's attempts to strike at his visual weakness. Purity in dress, speech, and conduct still matters to God. Purity in the life of Christians is supposed to be one of those distinguishing characteristics that convicts the world when they see it. They should be able to see it. Incidentally, the House of God used to be the safest place for a Christian man to be, but as it is now, he may be faced with far worse than what he would see in the world during the week. This should not be.

Matthew 5:8; 1 Timothy 2:9 & 10; 1 John 3:1-3; Psalm 51:10; James 4:7 & 8; Titus 2:11-13

Beloved, now we are children of God; and it has not yet been revealed what we shall be, but we know that when He is revealed, we shall be like Him, for we shall see Him as He is. And everyone who has this hope in Him purifies himself, just as He is pure. —1 John 3:2-3

Day 26

The reduction of God's Holy Spirit to goosebumps and gifts is disrespectful.

*B*y nature, we are emotionally driven. Our default is to make decisions and act according to what we feel. It takes great discipline and the work of God's Holy Spirit to help us master our emotions and whims. We call this maturing in Christ.

Emotions are not sinful; they are God-given. But they can mislead us, making us susceptible to error if they are not submitted to the Lordship of Christ. But sadly, many of us would rather massage our emotions than submit them, and as a result, we have conveniently reduced the purpose and power of God's Holy Spirit to gifts and how He makes us feel.

To balance our runaway emotions, we must return to the Word of God.

The Word teaches:
The Spirit testifies of Jesus.
He convicts the world of sin, righteousness, and judgment.
He reminds us of the words of Christ.
He guides us into all truth.
He glorifies Jesus.
The world cannot receive Him; it neither sees Him nor knows Him.
The Holy Spirit empowers us to preach the Gospel without regard for our lives.
He has given various gifts in the Body for our own edification and the edification of the Church.
He gives us undeniable boldness.

The Church was not advanced because they spoke in unknown languages. The Church was advanced because of the boldness of Spirit-filled believers who preached the cross at their own peril.

We didn't get the gospel today because of huddled Christians who came together to "feel" God. We got the gospel because the Holy Spirit's power motivated believers to esteem, preserve, and share it.

If you speak in unknown languages, cry uncontrollably during church, and feel goosebumps during the songs you like, but you're afraid to share the gospel or stand unapologetically on hard truths in the face of opposition, then go to your knees again. Ask the Lord to fill you with His Holy Spirit with the largely overlooked evidences of conviction of sin, guidance into truth, and boldness to preach the cross of Christ.

John 14:17; John 16; Acts 1:8, 4:23-31; 1 Corinthians 12, 13, & 14; 1 Timothy 1:7-12

But you shall receive power when the Holy Spirit has come upon you; and you shall be witnesses to Me in Jerusalem, and in all Judea and Samaria, and to the end of the earth.
–Acts 1:8

Day 27

The proof of loving God is in obeying Him.

*O*bedience is where the rubber meets the road in the lives of those professing Christianity. The slobbering love affair many have with the Lord ends when it comes to His "burdensome" commands. The Bible has so much to say about obedience, which means it's undeniably important to God. I would even venture to say obedience is the love language of God. We make huge errors by trying to love God on our terms, and we fail when we think we can love Him the way *we* feel loved. Obedience matters. It is a big, eternal deal.

Fellowship between the first man and God was broken because of disobedience, kings were dethroned because of disobedience, and professing believers show every day exactly whose they are because of disobedience. If we read the Word but don't do it, then we deceive ourselves. If the Holy Spirit leads us to end unhealthy relationships, change careers, or even hold a friend accountable and we don't do it, then we injure our relationship with the Lord. Obedience at every level, in *all* matters, is paramount.

History clearly shows that God does not accept partial obedience. God takes obedience very seriously. It is the number one external proof of submission to Him and His Lordship. No one who is truly in relationship with the Lord will exhibit pattern disobedience. At that point, we are likely discussing an apostate or an impostor.

Genesis 3:17; 1 Samuel 15:18-23; Luke 6:46-49; John 14:15, 23, 21, & 24; 2 John 1:6

He who has My commandments and keeps them, it is he who loves Me. And he who loves Me will be loved by My Father, and I will love him and manifest Myself to him.
–John 14:21

_____

_____

_____

_____

_____

_____

_____

_____

_____

_____

_____

_____

_____

_____

_____

_____

_____

_____

_____

_____

_____

_____

_____

_____

_____

_____

_____

_____

_____

Day 28

Pride is subtle.

*P*ride creeps into the life of the believer subtly at first, but left unchecked, it becomes more overt. The problem with pride is we most easily recognize it in the lives of others. The battle we fight against pride is ongoing and takes consistent and careful work. The ultimate offense of pride is that the created believes he has *anything* in which to boast. God hates pride—even the proud look. God, by the power of His Holy Spirit, is constantly searching us, and if we're willing, He is bringing to light even the subtle areas of pride in our lives.

We're prideful about ridiculous things: not being prideful, working hard for Jesus, giving, our looks, our knowledge of God's Word, our gifts and talents, what we wear, where we work, where we worship, the kids we have and how we raise them, or the kids we don't have.

One of the amazing things about pride is that all of us struggle with it. This particular sin is an imprint of the fall that is pre-wired into every one of us. Unlike fornication or lying, pride can take a while before we realize the damage it does to our relationship with God. Actually, in our pride we don't even notice that He has stepped back to allow us to reign in our own lives, seated on our own thrown. How dangerous!

The remedy for pride is not lowering our self-esteem— even that is an aim of the flesh. The remedy for pride is consistent fellowship with Jesus, whereby His Holy Spirit convicts us and allows siblings in Christ to challenge us. We must pay close attention to pride, for it makes us the object of God's opposition.

James 4:6-10; Galatians 6:3; 1 Corinthians 4:7; Psalm 10:4

The wicked in his proud countenance does not seek God;
God is in none of his thoughts. –Psalm 10:4

Day 29

A fixation with the "line of sin" often points to lack of fellow-ship/ relationship with the Lord.

*I*f I asked my husband, "What can I do with another man before you consider it cheating or crossing the line?" he might rightly be offended. In fact, any decent friend might point out how ridiculous the question is and that it reveals something about the position of my heart toward my husband.

God has parameters and boundaries for His people that display His great love and protection for us. They also point to the type of discipline He expects and the holiness He requires. The problem for many of us when it comes to seeking to please God is that we ask the ridiculous question, "How close can I get to the line of sin without crossing it?"

The aim of the believer is to live nowhere near the line. The aim of the believer is to desperately desire to please the Lord in all our doing. The Bible contains some real black-and-white dos and don'ts, but disputable or doubtful matters also exist. These matters and areas that are not expressly laid out provide opportunities for our hearts to be revealed. The question is, "What does our preoccupation with the 'line of sin' say about our fellowship with Christ?"

I love my husband, and I would never consider what I could get away with when it comes to the integrity of our marital relationship. Likewise, we as the Bride of Christ must do away with seeking to discover how close we can get to the line of sin and still be approved by God.

1 Thessalonians 4:1-8; Colossians 3:1-11; Romans 13:11-14

Let us walk properly, as in the day, not in revelry and drunkenness, not in lewdness and lust, not in strife and envy. But put on the Lord Jesus Christ, and make no provision for the flesh, to fulfill its lusts. –Romans13:13 & 14

_____

_____

_____

_____

_____

_____

_____

_____

_____

_____

_____

_____

_____

_____

_____

_____

_____

_____

_____

_____

_____

_____

_____

_____

_____

_____

_____

_____

Day 30

"Follow your heart" is an encouragement Satan whispers.

From outside the Church have come all sorts of practices and encouragements that should have stayed where they were. Unfortunately, much of the new age, secular self-help the world cherishes has seeped inside. It has confused many believers because many false teachers have mixed it with biblical application. Woe to them.

One such popular practice or encouragement is that of teaching believers to "follow your heart." Ugh! This is so far from biblical that it's almost wicked. The heart deceives us. The heart, in conjunction with our flesh, wants what's contrary to the will of God. It hides and treasures sin. We have to watch the heart and keep tight reins on it. The heart will mislead us. The heart makes snap decisions that the mind is left to clean up. Even a heart submitted to the Lordship of Christ must fight daily to honor God; how much more a heart encouraged to take the lead.

No – don't follow your heart; follow the Spirit of the living God. Following the Spirit of God actually identifies you as a child of God—a distinction not noted about the heart. When it comes to surefire ways to walk contrary to Jesus, following your heart ranks right up there with "believing in yourself," "doing you," and "living your truth." All of these admonishments/ encouragements are rooted in the worship and exaltation of self. They have no place among the called out of God, much less being propagated in the Church.

Jeremiah 17:9; Proverbs 23:7, 26:23-25; Romans 8:14

For as many as are led by the Spirit of God, these are sons of God. –Romans 8:14
"The heart is deceitful above all things,
And desperately wicked;
Who can know it? –Jeremiah 17:9

_____

_____

_____

_____

_____

_____

_____

_____

_____

_____

_____

_____

_____

_____

_____

_____

_____

_____

_____

_____

_____

_____

_____

_____

_____

_____

_____

_____

Day 31

God is not on our side until we're on His.

*T*he invitation from Jesus to His disciples was, "Follow me, and I will make you become fishers of men." The call was never, "Let me follow you." Usually when I've heard people remind themselves that God is on their side, it's been amidst struggles or problems. They don't fear what's going to happen because, "God is on my side."

What if I said, "No, He isn't?" At least not in the sense we've come to believe.

The truth is we who are believers are on *His* side. We are the ones who cross over from death to life. This may be a subtle distinction, but it's an important one.

The danger of the pop culture notion that God is on *our* side is the real temptation to live like He is just along for the ride that is our life. However, when we believe we have crossed the line of death and destruction to stand on the Lord's side, we live in submission to Him. We walk after Him, not before Him. The position of being on the Lord's side speaks of abandoning our side, our will, our plans, and our desires and taking up His plan, His will, and His desires. Who is preeminent? Who is above all? Who is the first and the last? It's the Lord! Because of that and so much more, He gets top billing.

The Christian is on the Lord's side. It is the *only* side that matters.

Exodus 32:26; Colossians 1:18; John 3:31

*then Moses stood in the entrance of the camp, and said,
"Whoever is on theLord's side—come to me!" And all the
sons of Levi gathered themselves together to him.*
–Exodus 32:26

_____

_____

_____

_____

_____

_____

_____

_____

_____

_____

_____

_____

_____

_____

_____

_____

_____

_____

_____

_____

_____

_____

_____

_____

_____

_____

_____

_____

Conclusion

*T*he Lord is worthy that we should delight in His hard truths. As the world pushes more aggressively against the Church, we must not give in. Too often, instead of the Church responding to secular cultural shifts with truth, we've incorporated those shifts into our weekly gatherings. Sadly for the lost, there is little distinction between the called out of God and those marked for destruction. How can we ever expect to win the lost when we present to them a god they themselves have created?

The world doesn't mind our Christ if they can add Him to everything else. The world doesn't mind Scripture when it's presented as one thought or concept among many. However when we rightly communicate Christ in absolute terms and uphold the Word as non-negotiable, the followers diminish dramatically. We, those willing to stand in this final stretch, must be able to assert, as Elijah did on Mount Carmel, "How long will you falter between two opinions? If the Lord is God, follow Him; but if Baal, follow him." These hard truths and the countless others contained in the Bible are for those willing to follow the Lord.